Newton
AND
GRAVITY

by Stephanie Wilder

PEARSON
Scott
Foresman

DK

What You Already Know

Relative motion is a change in one object's position compared to another object's position. You can judge relative motion based on your frame of reference. Suppose you are riding in a car. You pass houses and trees. You can tell that you are moving by the objects you pass. Houses do not move relative to you in the car. Your position in the car is your frame of reference.

Speed is a measure of how quickly an object moves. Velocity is a measure of both the speed of an object and the direction in which it moves.

A force is any push or pull. Force can make an object stand still or move forward or backward. The object moves in the same direction as the force acting on it. All forces have size and direction.

An object that is not moving will not start moving unless a force acts on it. Inertia is an object's resistance to any change to its motion.

Friction can play a role in the movement of an object. The more friction there is between objects, the more energy is needed to make them move. Smooth objects don't need a lot of force to move, but rough ones do. Objects with less mass move more easily than objects with more mass.

Work is the ability to move something. Work requires energy. Kinetic energy is the energy of motion. All moving things have kinetic energy. Potential energy is stored energy.

Gravity is the force that pulls two objects toward each other. Gravity is stronger if objects are closer together.

The study of gravity is just one scientific area in which Isaac Newton made a contribution. He made many discoveries that are still used by scientists today.

Newton's study of gravity has made rides such as roller coasters possible.

Isaac Newton

Isaac Newton was born at Woolsthorpe Manor in England on January 4, 1643. Newton was a clever child. He loved to build model windmills and mechanical toys.

Isaac Newton

Newton was not very good at looking after the family farm. So when he was old enough, Newton went to Trinity College at the University of Cambridge to study.

Newton's birthplace

Newton studied at Trinity College in Cambridge, England.

At Cambridge, Newton was an average student. He had trouble understanding the works of the ancient Greek scientists he studied in his classes. But on his own, Newton read books by more modern scientists.

In 1665, a terrible disease swept across England. The University of Cambridge was closed to keep the students from getting sick. In the eighteen months that Newton stayed home from Cambridge, he made his three greatest scientific discoveries. He invented a new kind of math, made discoveries about the relationship between light and color, and came up with the beginning of his theory of gravity. Although Newton would continue to do important work for the rest of his life, these were his greatest achievements.

Scientific Genius

Isaac Newton studied many areas of science. He studied the science behind rainbows. He discovered that white light is made up of all the colors of the spectrum. He also found that white light can be separated into these colors using a prism. When white light goes through a prism, or even a raindrop, you can see all of its colors.

Newton's experiments with prisms contributed to his knowledge of the spectrum.

Newton invented the first reflecting telescope.

Newton used all that he had learned from his study of prisms to build the first reflecting telescope. This was a telescope that used mirrors instead of glass lenses. It was more powerful than other telescopes of the time. Now people could study the stars more closely than ever before.

Newton described three laws of motion. His first law of motion is that an object in motion will stay in motion unless acted on by an outside force. That means a ball rolling across the floor will keep rolling until a force, such as friction, makes it stop.

The second law of motion explains how force, mass, and movement are related. If two balls have the same mass but one is moving faster, the faster ball will have more force. If the balls are moving at the same speed but one has more mass, the ball with more mass will have more force.

Newton's third law states that when you use force on an object, it uses an equal but opposite force on you. If you stub your toe on a rock, your toe will hurt. This is due to the force of the rock pushing back.

According to Newton's third law, the space shuttle moves up with the same amount of force as that of the rocket engines pushing down.

What is gravity?

Newton stated that gravity is a force that pulls two objects together. Every object has gravity. The pull of an object's gravity depends on the mass of the object and the distance between it and another object. Newton put this idea into his famous book, *Principia*.

The gravitational pull of Earth is very strong. It is this force that pulls you and everything around you toward the center of Earth.

Earth has a powerful gravitational pull.

Perhaps Newton came up with the idea for the theory of gravity after watching an apple fall to the ground from a tree.

Though not recorded officially, many claim that Newton discovered gravity while observing an apple tree. An apple fell from the tree and hit the ground. Newton wondered what made that apple drop to the ground instead of float away.

Then he started to think about the force that keeps the Moon orbiting Earth. Newton knew that objects tend to move in straight paths. So why didn't the Moon move in a straight line off into space? Newton realized that Earth has to be pulling on the Moon to keep it from flying away. This pulling force is gravity. Newton used his math skills to prove that the force that makes the apple fall to the ground is the same force that keeps the Moon in its orbit of Earth.

Weight and Mass

Mass is the amount of matter in an object. On Earth, gravity pulls on mass and makes it move toward the center of Earth. Weight depends on gravity. Weight is the measure of gravity's pull on an object.

If you climb to the top of a tall mountain, your weight will be a tiny bit less than it was at the foot of the mountain. This is because gravity gets weaker as objects get farther apart. At the foot of the mountain, you are closer to Earth's gravitational pull. At the top of the mountain, you are farther away from that pull. Think about a small magnet and a paper clip. The magnet can move the clip when they are close together. But from across the room, the magnet isn't strong enough to move the clip. The magnet's pull decreases with distance.

You weigh slightly less at the top of a mountain.

Gravity also depends on an object's mass. Objects with more mass have more gravity. Earth has much more mass than the Moon. The force of gravity on the Moon is much less than the force of gravity on Earth. If you went to the Moon, your mass would not change. But your weight would change. The Moon's weaker gravity would not pull on you as hard as Earth's strong gravity does. This means you would weigh less.

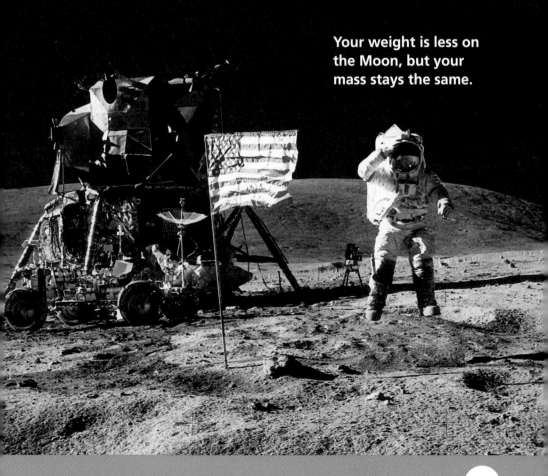

Your weight is less on the Moon, but your mass stays the same.

Earth and Moon

Earth pulls on the Moon, keeping it on its path around Earth. The force of gravity keeps the Moon in its orbit. Suppose you are swinging around a ball on a string. You are Earth. The ball is the Moon, and the string is gravity. If you keep holding the string, the ball must keep moving around you. In the same way, as long as there is gravity, the Moon will keep moving around Earth. What if you let go of the string? The ball would fly away from you. The same thing would happen if gravity weren't holding the Moon in place. The Moon would spin away from Earth.

At the same time as Earth is pulling on the Moon, the Moon pulls on Earth. This causes the daily tides in the ocean.

Newton applied his theory of gravity to the tides he saw every day. The part of the ocean that is underneath the Moon is pulled up by the Moon's gravity. This causes high tides. At high tide, water levels rise and more water moves onto the shore. As the water moves toward the Moon, it is pulled away from other areas. These areas experience low tide. At low tide, water levels drop and water moves away from the shore.

During high tide, water is pulled toward the shore.

During low tide, water is pulled away from the shore.

The Sun and Planets

All planets in the solar system orbit around the Sun. The Sun holds them in orbit, just as Earth holds the Moon in orbit. Gravity keeps the planets in their orbits. Without gravity, the planets might go hurtling off into space. Newton used his theory of gravity to explain why the planets go around the Sun in an elliptical, or oval, path.

The Sun and planets are controlled by gravity.

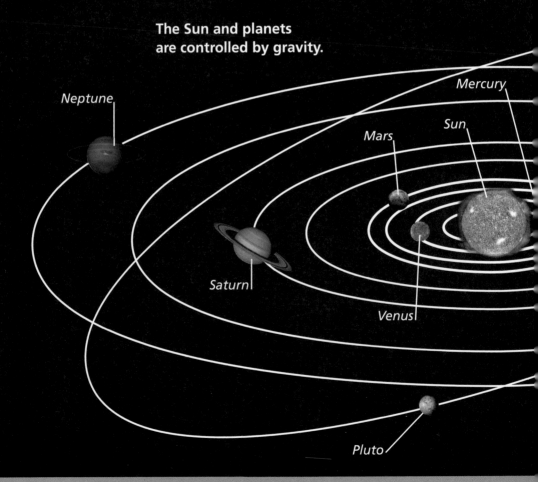

Neptune

Mercury

Mars

Sun

Saturn

Venus

Pluto

Sir Isaac Newton grew up to be one of the most important scientists of all time. His laws of motion and his theory of gravity have helped scientists understand the universe better. Without his scientific contributions, we would not be able to explore space. Newton would be proud to know that his work has allowed future generations to explore the galaxy that he was only able to see through a telescope.

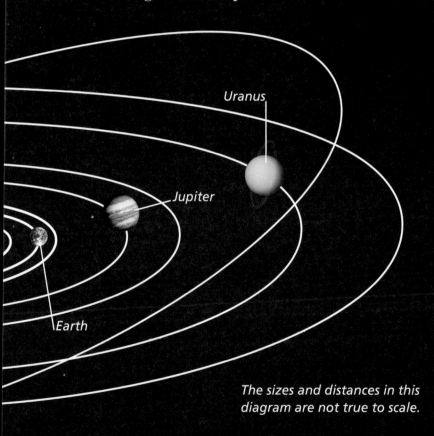

Uranus

Jupiter

Earth

The sizes and distances in this diagram are not true to scale.

Glossary

elliptical   having the shape of an oval

gravitational pull   the pull on an object caused
                          by gravity

prism   a transparent solid that can
                          separate white light into all
                          colors

reflecting telescope a powerful telescope that uses
                          mirrors instead of glass lenses

spectrum   a band of colors formed when
                          a beam of light passes through
                          a prism

tides   the alternate rise and fall of the
                          surface of the oceans connected
                          and bodies of water

white light   light that is made up of all the
                          colors of the spectrum